T0362669

BADASS MUMS

30 BOUNDARY BREAKING WOMEN GETTING $#*! DONE

Affirm press

Affirmpress
books that leave an impression

Published by Affirm Press in 2019
28 Thistlethwaite Street, South Melbourne, VIC 3205
www.affirmpress.com.au
10 9 8 7 6 5 4 3 2 1

A catalogue record for this
book is available from the
National Library of Australia

Title: Badass Mums
ISBN: 9781925870190 (hardback)

Cover design and illustration by Sarah Firth
Internal design by Sinéad Murphy
Proudly printed in China by 1010 Printing

Every effort has been made to ensure that the facts presented in this book are
correct. Any new information supplied will be included in subsequent editions.

Aboriginal and Torres Strait Islander readers are advised that this book contains
images and names of deceased persons.

To Dr Dianne Firth OAM, Dr Frances Dark,
and Robyn Bishop (1949 – 2018)
– the most badass mums of all.

ROLL OF HONORARY
BADASSES

Ann Jarvis

Azucena Villaflor

Waris Dirie

Jin Xing

Erma Bombeck

Evonne Goolagong Cawley

Aishwarya Rai Bachchan

Irena Sendler

Patti Smith

Jessica Walton

Daphne Ceeney

Wangari Muta Maathai

Helen Garner

Aretha Franklin

Catherine Hamlin

Debbie Reynolds & Carrie Fisher

Penny Wong

Mum Shirl

Serena Williams

Nancy Edison

Jane Goodall

JK Rowling

Ameera Ahmad Harouda

Valentina Tereshkova

Cate Blanchett

Amanda Palmer

Fanny Blankers-Koen

Angie Xtravaganza

Jacinda Ardern

BADASS MUMS

INTRODUCTION

In books about incredible women the usual suspects make the rounds: Frida Kahlo, Amelia Earhart, Mary MacKillop, Virginia Woolf, and so on. Now, there's no disputing the 'rebel' status of these women, or that their work was amazing, but you might have noticed something interesting: most of them never had children. And as they dominate the lists of 'top women in history' over and over, you'd be forgiven for thinking that it's just not possible to be a mother *and* change the world. Well, it's time to smash that myth to pieces.

Let's be real, being a woman is tough, and being a mother tougher still. This book shines a light on a diverse range of trailblazing women who've fought, run, danced, sung and thought their way to the top of their fields, all while being badass mums. From the mothers working and raising families against the odds, to the record-breaking women who refused to stick to the status quo, this is a celebration of just some of the women who are championing unique approaches to motherhood. After all, there's nothing more badass than being a mum.

Ann Jarvis

SOCIAL ACTIVIST

Ann Jarvis

> '[I] hope and pray that someone, sometime, will found a memorial mother's day commemorating her for the matchless service she renders to humanity in every field of life.'

— ANNA JARVIS SPEAKING OF HER MOTHER

Did you ever wonder how Mother's Day started? With a badass mum, of course! In the 19th century, poor sanitary conditions and a lack of proper medical assistance made childbirth dangerous. Ann Jarvis had thirteen children, but tragically only four survived to adulthood. A dynamic, community-minded woman, Ann took her grief and channelled it into helping mothers in need. Ann instigated Mothers' Day Work Clubs, which raised money for medicine and care in an effort to reduce infant mortality rates.

During the American Civil War, the focus of the clubs shifted to promote peace and compassion for all, offering aid to both Confederate and Union soldiers. Ann's social activism continued after the war when she organised a 'Mothers' Friendship Day' for soldiers from both sides and their families.

After Ann's death in 1905, her daughter Anna was so inspired by her mother's generosity that she began advocating for a national holiday to honour mothers. In 1914, President Woodrow Wilson officially declared the second Sunday in May the national Mother's Day in the United States. It is important to remember that Mother's Day isn't all about flowers and corny cards: it's about honouring the hard work and compassion that goes into being a mum.

Azucena Villaflor

FOUNDER OF THE MOTHERS OF THE PLAZA
DE MAYO MOVEMENT

Azucena Villaflor

'She was like the mother hen who watched out for all of us.'

– HISTORIAN ENRIQUE ARROSAGARAY

Azucena Villaflor was 'nothing more than a housewife' according to her daughter. But this humble housewife became an unlikely hero in Argentina after she founded the Mothers of the Plaza de Mayo movement, a human rights group dedicated to finding missing persons following Argentina's 'Dirty War'.

From 1976 to 1983, an estimated 30,000 citizens of Argentina were abducted and sometimes killed by the ruling military regime. Néstor De Vicenti, Azucena's eldest son, disappeared in November 1976. He was never seen again. In her grief Azucena made a decision that would turn her from housewife to hero. On 30 April 1977, Azucena and thirteen other mothers whose loved ones were also among the *desaparecidos* – the 'disappeared' – met in the Plaza de Mayo in the centre of Buenos Aires. They wore white headscarves bearing the names of their missing children. Every Thursday thereafter, the group met to demand information on their lost children. Public demonstrations were forbidden by the regime, so this was a dangerous move. In 1977, Azucena was abducted; her body was later found washed up on a beach.

The courage of Azucena and the Mothers was contagious. They inspired women across the globe, and their white scarves became an international symbol of democratic resistance.

Waris Dirie

MODEL AND ANTI-FGM ACTIVIST

Waris Dirie

'I just knew that I had to tell the world that there was torture, an undercover war against women. But this is not one person's war – all of us have to do something.'

– WARIS IN AN INTERVIEW IN THE *GUARDIAN*

Growing up in the Somalian desert, Waris Dirie was just five years old when she was subjected to the cruel practice of female genital mutilation (FGM). Then, at age 13, she ran away from home to escape an arranged marriage to a man in his sixties. She trekked barefoot across the desert with almost nothing to eat or drink. 'I knew that as long as I was alive, I could make it,' she told *Harper's Bazaar* in 2010. 'I had nothing to lose but my freedom.'

Waris eventually travelled to London, where she worked as a maid and at McDonald's. When she was 18, she was discovered by fashion photographer Terence Donovan and went on to become one of the first African supermodels, gracing the catwalks of New York, Milan and Paris – she even appeared in a James Bond film. She retired from modelling in 1997 when her son, Aleeke, was born.

Revealing her incredible story of survival in her autobiography, *Desert Flower,* Waris became the voice of the voiceless, using her profile to raise awareness of the horrors of FGM. In 2002, Waris founded her own organisation, called the Desert Flower Foundation, which has assisted more than 40,000 girls who have been affected by or are at risk of FGM. She was appointed as a UN Special Ambassador and in 2019 was named as one the Sunhak Peace Prize laureates.

Jin Xing

TALK-SHOW HOST

Jin Xing

'Some people criticised me: "... How does she have a right to be raising kids?" I said, "Shut up. Am I a good mother or not?"'

- JIN XING IN AN INTERVIEW WITH *HOLLYWOOD REPORTER*

Known as the 'Oprah of China', former ballet dancer and army colonel Jin Xing was the first public figure in China to undergo gender reassignment surgery and one of the first transgender women to be officially recognised as a woman by the government of China. With her unique story and immense popularity, Jin Xing has become an icon in the changing Chinese cultural landscape.

Gaining both national and international prominence through her dancing career, Jin underwent gender reassignment surgery in Beijing at the age of 28. She then established a dance company and adopted three children who she raised as a single mother until her marriage to Heinz-Gerd Oidtmann in 2005.

She later became the host of *The Jin Xing Show*, which attracted an estimated 100 million viewers weekly. While she still faces criticism for being transgender, public support since Jin first began transitioning over twenty years ago reveals the potential for social attitudes to change. 'When I did the gender reassignment surgery two decades ago, only 30 per cent of people sided with me,' Jin told the *South China Morning Post*. 'Nowadays, I think about 80 per cent of people recognise my choice.' However, when asked in interviews about the criticism she's faced, Jin always points out that her family's opinion, and that of her three children in particular, is the only thing she cares about.

Erma Bombeck

COLUMNIST

Erma Bombeck

'Giving birth is little more than a set of muscular contractions granting passage of a child. Then the mother is born.'

- ERMA BOMBECK

....

Erma Bombeck was the housewife whose writing left a whole nation in stitches. Erma started by writing humorous columns for her Ohio high school, before beginning a weekly column called 'At Wit's End' for the local *Kettering-Oakwood Times* in 1964. She was only paid $3 for each column, but even badass mums have to start somewhere.

Writing from her house in the middle of suburbia, Erma's columns captured the day-to-day struggles of motherhood. As a stay-at-home mum with three children, she had plenty of material to draw from. Motherhood was her beat; she wrote about everything from meat loaf and misplaced socks, to depression, sex and empty-nesting. Her witty and refreshingly honest writing style soon saw her landing million-dollar book deals. Her column went from appearing once a week in a local paper to running three times a week in nine hundred newspapers across America. In a time when women were pressured to maintain a 'nuclear family', Erma reminded them that life was full of ups and downs, and that was okay.

Once describing herself as 'a pair of white socks in a pantyhose world', Erma Bombeck was one of the most successful female humorists of the 20th century. Yes, Erma agreed that motherhood was a gift, but it was also a bloody tough time and what could we do but laugh!

Evonne Goolagong Cawley

AUSTRALIAN TENNIS LEGEND

Evonne Goolagong Cawley

> 'Her story is even more remarkable because she is one of very few women who have won a major tournament as a mother.'
>
> **– JOANNE BACH, NATIONAL MUSEUM AUSTRALIA CURATOR**

....

Wiradjuri Aboriginal Australian and tennis champion Evonne Goolagong Cawley is one of the most significant figures in Australia's sporting history. Named the number one female player in the world in 1971 and 1976, Evonne won seven Grand Slams across her career, including two Wimbledon victories. Most notably, Evonne's second Wimbledon triumph, in 1980, made her the first mother since 1914 – and the second overall – to win the title.

Following her retirement in 1983, Evonne continued to be an ambassador for tennis and Indigenous sport, receiving countless awards for her accomplishments and service to the community. From 1997 to 2001, Evonne also acted as a consultant for the Federal Government, forming The Evonne Goolagong Sports Trust to review Aboriginal sports facilities and raise funds for new facilities. She was admitted into the International Tennis Hall of Fame in 1988.

In 2012, Evonne founded the Evonne Goolagong Foundation, which aims to utilise tennis 'as a vehicle to attract Indigenous girls and boys in order to promote and help provide quality education and better health through diet and exercise'. Her daughter Kelly works alongside her mother in the organisation, helping to run tennis camps.

Aishwarya Rai Bachchan

BOLLYWOOD STAR

Aishwarya Rai Bachchan

'But of course, the absolute unknown, most beautiful and blessed out learning phase has been motherhood.'

- AISHWARYA INTERVIEWED IN *DNAINDIA*

Easily one of the finest and most acclaimed Bollywood actresses, former Miss World Aishwarya Rai Bachchan has starred in over 47 films since her acting debut in 1997. Often referred to as one of the most beautiful women in the world, Aishwarya is known for both her cinematic accomplishments and her significant contribution to humanitarian causes, and in 2009 was bestowed with the Padma Shri, the fourth-highest civilian honour given by the Indian Government.

In 2011, Aishwarya and her husband, fellow Bollywood actor Abhishek Bachchan, became parents for the first time to their daughter, Aaradhya. Aishwarya was at the height of her career yet chose to take a break from acting to be a full-time mother.

She has recently returned to film work and in interviews will frequently stress the importance of fostering an understanding in her daughter of her role as a working mum: 'I do refer to my filming locations as an office, because I want Aaradhya to understand that I am a working mother ... because that's what it should be.'

Irena Sendler

WAR HERO

Irena Sendler

'To me and many rescued children, Irena Sendler is a third mother. Good, wise, kind, always accepting, she shares our happiness and worries.'

- ELZBIETA FICOWSKA, ONE OF THE CHILDREN SAVED BY IRENA

Known as the 'mother of the Holocaust children', Polish social worker Irena Sendler helped rescue 2500 Jewish children from the Warsaw Ghetto.

When the Warsaw Ghetto was established in 1940, Irena's position as a social worker granted her regular access into the largest ghetto in Poland, and she soon became a member of an underground group called Zegota – or 'the Council to Aid Jews'. Irena and fellow members of Zegota worked to rescue as many children as possible by smuggling them out of the ghetto through caskets, potato sacks, ambulances or through underground tunnels, and then placing them with non-Jewish families. Her plan was to reunite the rescued children with their parents after the war, but the majority of the parents did not survive.

Following the war, Irena's first marriage ended in divorce. She remarried in 1947 and had three children. In 2008, Irena died in Warsaw aged 98. Following her passing, her daughter Janina stated, 'To me, my mother's story shows that you are not aware what you are capable of – either for good or for bad – until a critical moment comes.'

Patti Smith

THE GODMOTHER OF PUNK

Patti Smith

'I was still a worker. Some people said, "Oh, well, you didn't do anything in the 80s" – first of all, to be a mother and a wife is probably the hardest job one can have.'

– PATTI SMITH INTERVIEWED IN THE *GUARDIAN*

Patti Smith constantly defied expectations as a musician and writer, and confirmed that there is nothing more punk than being a mum. After her first album, *Horses*, Patti quickly became a legend in the New York City punk rock scene. *Horses* would go on to influence the likes of The Smiths and PJ Harvey.

She took fans by surprise when she semi-retired from music to raise her two children, Jackson and Jesse, in suburban Detroit. Many people criticised her at the time, viewing her decision as a betrayal of feminism, an admission that women couldn't 'have it all'; she was labelled a 'sell-out' and a 'domestic cow'. But Patti knew that she was making the right decision for herself as a mother, and for her children. 'I just felt it was time for me to develop myself in other areas,' she said. 'I don't think touring and children mix.'

During her years in Detroit, Patti never stopped writing and creating. She would write for three hours every morning before her children woke up. Patti made her musical comeback in the 90s, and in 2010 she won the National Book Award for her incredible memoir, *Just Kids*. Patti showed us that motherhood and creativity aren't mutually exclusive. Now, she is able to take to the stage alongside her children who are also musicians, proving that actually, yes, women can have it all (especially if they're badass).

Jessica Walton

PICTURE BOOK AUTHOR

Jessica Walton

'If kids have bookshelves full of the same kind of family ... they'll get the message that that family is the normal one, and anything else is 'other'. I decided to write the book I needed for my family.'

- JESSICA INTERVIEWED IN *BETTER READING*

When Jessica Walton couldn't find a picture book for her son that represented her family, she took things into her own hands. Jessica's dad, Tina, came out as transgender later in life and became the co-founder of Gender Diversity Australasia. Not long after this, Jessica married her wife – before the legalisation of same-sex marriage in Australia – and together they had a son. But upon discovering that there simply wasn't anything about gender identity in picture books, she launched a Kickstarter campaign to create her own story.

In 2016, Jessica was able to write and publish *Introducing Teddy,* a heartwarming story about a trans teddy coming out to her family. The book honoured Tina, and allowed Jessica's son to see a family like his own represented on the page.

Jessica not only created a representation of her own loved ones, but also helped other trans children and family members feel less isolated by celebrating the happy families that come in all shapes and sizes.

Jessica continues to fight for representation in literature through her work as a writer, teacher, musician and mother. After losing her leg to cancer at the age of nine, she is also a strong advocate for disability rights and representation. Could she be any more badass?

Daphne Ceeney

PARALYMPIAN

Daphne Ceeney

'Daphne shone a light on a path for all women with disabilities in this country to reach for the very best in themselves.'

– DANIELA DI TORO, CO-CAPTAIN OF THE 2016 AUSTRALIAN PARALYMPIC TEAM

Daphne Ceeney was one of Australia's most dedicated and pioneering athletes. She was the first woman to compete in the Paralympic Games, winning a career total of 14 medals across swimming, table tennis, athletics, archery and fencing. Talk about multi-talented!

Growing up in the town of Harden-Murrumburrah, New South Wales, Daphne was 17 when she broke her back in a horse-riding accident and became paraplegic. But not even this life-altering injury could dampen her enthusiasm for sport; during rehabilitation she set her sights on the Paralympic Games. At the time, sport for people with disabilities was dominated by men, but that didn't stop Daphne. In 1960, she was the only Australian female athlete in the Paralympics in Rome, and she ended up winning six of Australia's ten medals. Daphne went on to compete in three Paralympics between 1960 and 1968.

On becoming pregnant with twins, Daphne applied the same fierce determination she'd shown on the sporting stage to her impending role as a mum. Once more she defied assumptions about what her body was capable of, spending six months in hospital in order to safely deliver her children. Daphne Ceeney didn't let anything deter her from her dreams of being an athlete or a mother. She will be remembered as a true trailblazer.

Wangari Muta Maathai

NOBEL LAUREATE

Wangari Muta Maathai

'The fact that one woman ... could be such a
potent force for change remains one of the most
inspiring things for me.'

- WANJIRA MATHAI, WANGARI'S DAUGHTER, IN AN INTERVIEW WITH THE BBC

Kenyan environmental warrior Wangari Muta Maathai fought tirelessly for environmental conservation and the rights of women. In 2004, she became the first African woman to receive the Nobel Peace Prize.

After earning a scholarship to study in the United States, Wangari completed a Masters in Biological Science. She then pursued her Doctorate, first studying in Germany and later returning to Nairobi as an assistant lecturer. In 1971, as a mother of two, she became the first woman in east and central Africa to obtain a PhD from an African university.

In 1977, Wangari formed the grassroots organisation the Green Belt Movement, which worked towards bettering the lives of African women through land protection and community tree-planting initiatives. This movement resulted in the planting of over 30 million trees across Kenya and provided an estimated 30,000 women with new skills.

Wangari was a tireless advocate for women and the environment until her death in 2011. Wangari's children continue her good work: her eldest daughter, Wanjira, is the Chairperson of the Green Belt Movement, and her son, Waweru, is a founding member of the Wangari Maathai Foundation.

Helen Garner

LITERARY LEGEND

B. 1942, AUSTRALIA

Helen Garner

'The best thing that's ever happened to me, bar none, is having grandchildren and living by them and being part of their lives.'

- HELEN GARNER

Helen Garner was born in Geelong, Victoria, and raised in an 'ordinary Australian home – not many books and not much talk'. An intellectually curious and adventurous person from a young age, Helen sought out books and art in her university years, studying English and French before becoming a teacher.

Never one to toe the stuffy, traditional line, Helen was sacked by the Victorian Department of Education after a lesson in Ancient Greek turned into an impromptu sex education class, where Helen promised to answer her students' questions honestly and accurately. In 1977, she went on to write her first novel, *Monkey Grip*, now considered an Australian classic. Helen's subsequent books have won countless awards, making her one of the most important and original voices in Australian literature.

Helen raised her daughter, Alice, among artists and academics in communal households, the stark opposite of Helen's own childhood home. Helen championed an unconventional upbringing for Alice, promoting independence and respect between mother and daughter. Years later their mutual respect and admiration is going strong: they even live side-by-side and Helen often pops by to help raise Alice's young children. Helen Garner is not only a badass mum, but also a badass grandma.

Aretha Franklin

QUEEN OF SOUL

B. 1942, UNITED STATES

Aretha Franklin

'My children have been wonderful. Times when they have been down, they lifted me up.'

– ARETHA IN AN INTERVIEW WITH *EBONY*

....

The powerful soul singer Aretha Franklin was just 12 when she became pregnant with her first son. She was a mother of two by the time she was 14. While her talent as a musician was profound even as a child – at seven, she could replay a tune on a piano after hearing it once – Aretha's early life, according to her sister Erma, was rough and led to a life of 'silent suffering'.

Aretha was 19 when she married her first husband, Ted White, and when her first hit 'Won't be Long' charted in the Top 100. The young mother had her third son, Ted Jnr, with White. However, their marriage was short-lived due to White's abusive behaviour. Her youngest son, Kecalf, was born in 1970 with her road manager, Ken Cunningham.

Despite her rough beginnings, Aretha achieved icon status. Her songs became anthems for women around the world fighting for respect, independence and recognition. 'We can all learn a little something from each other, so whatever people can take and be inspired by where my music is concerned is great,' she told *Time*. In 1987, she became the first woman inducted into the Rock and Roll Hall of Fame and was given the Presidential Medal of Freedom in 2005. Aretha will be remembered as an unparalleled talent who inspired women around the world to demand R.E.S.P.E.C.T.

Catherine Hamlin

PIONEERING OBSTETRICIAN

Catherine Hamlin

'Catherine has only one son, but she has 35,000 daughters.'

– RICHARD HAMLIN, SPEAKING ON HIS MOTHER'S 90TH BIRTHDAY.

....

Recognised as a pioneer in fistula surgery by the United Nations Population Fund and twice nominated for the Nobel Peace Prize, Dr Catherine Hamlin's immense contribution to the field of gynaecology means that over 50,000 women living in poverty have received treatment for severe childbirth injuries.

In 1959, Catherine moved to Ethiopia with her husband, Reginald, a fellow doctor, and their six-year-old son, Richard. They arrived at the behest of the Ethiopian government, as part of a three-year contract to work as gynaecologists and to develop a midwifery school. Shocked by the lack of treatment available to women suffering with obstetric fistula, a serious medical condition where a hole develops in the birth canal, the couple chose to stay on in Ethiopia after their three-year contract was up to focus on treating these kinds of injuries.

Today, the couple's vision has expanded into the Hamlin Fistula Ethiopia healthcare network, which has established five regional fistula hospitals across Ethiopia, as well as 40 Hamlin Midwifery Clinics and the Hamlin College of Midwives. Catherine has received many awards during her 55-year career, including the Order of Australia, the Right Livelihood Award and the Centenary Medal. Her son, Richard, who is also a doctor, now carries on his parents' work in the organisation they founded.

Debbie Reynolds and Carrie Fisher

HOLLYWOOD ROYALTY

Debbie Reynolds and Carrie Fisher

'If I'm like her in any way then I'm very, very happy that I am.'

– CARRIE FISHER SPEAKING OF HER MOTHER

Debbie Reynolds and Carrie Fisher showed us how strong and deep-rooted the connection is between a badass mother and a badass daughter. Debbie, an actress best known for her role in *Singin' in the Rain*, raised Carrie in the glitz and glamour of Hollywood. Later Carrie would follow her mother into showbiz, landing the role as Princess Leia in *Star Wars*.

As close as they were, the pair had their ups and downs, including a period of estrangement around the time Carrie struggled with addiction and bipolar disorder. Carrie wrote about her mental health in *Wishful Drinking*, and fought to change the harmful stigma around mental illness. Her advocacy, scorching wisecracks and hilarious honesty made her beloved around the world. 'If my life wasn't funny, it would just be true,' Carrie wrote, 'and that is unacceptable.'

When Carrie and Debbie reconnected, they were a force to be reckoned with. Along with Carrie's daughter, Billie Lourd, who is also an actress, they continued to be a close and loving showbiz family. When Carrie suddenly passed away at 60, Debbie followed her a day later. Those close to Debbie say that she died of a broken heart, noting that one of the last things she said was, 'I want to be with Carrie.' Their legacy as a fearless and dynamic duo is an inspiration to mothers and daughters everywhere.

Penny Wong

AUSTRALIAN SENATOR

Penny Wong

'I want my daughters to grow into strong women who have the opportunity to achieve anything they set their minds to.'

– PENNY IN THE *HERALD SUN*

....

Penny Ying-Yen Wong cuts a badass figure in Australian politics: she's the first openly gay federal female politician in Australia, the first woman to be Leader of the Government in the Senate and the first Asian-born Cabinet minister.

Penny was born in Kota Kinabalu, Malaysia, and moved to Australia with her family when she was eight. In 2001, she was elected to represent South Australia in the Senate. As a member of the Labor Party, she has spent time as a member of the Government and in opposition. Penny has two daughters with her partner, Sophie Allouache. She keeps most of her family life private, but she brought Allouache to her first Senatorial swearing-in ceremony because she wanted to be open about her relationship. 'Being open about it was a statement in itself,' she said. 'Normalising being different is important, because being different is okay.'

During the same-sex marriage debate in 2017, Wong campaigned for a yes vote. 'Thank you for standing up for equality,' she said, when the public referendum returned a resounding YES. 'Thank you for standing up for our families.'

From a small town in Malaysia to the head of the Australian Senate, the trailblazing Penny Wong shows us how mums can challenge the status quo and create a better society for their children.

Mum Shirl

WELFARE WORKER

Mum Shirl

'Mum Shirl always had a concern for people who had nowhere to sleep ... She would run around to make sure they were all right.'

- DR ROBERTA SYKES

Mum Shirl, born Colleen Shirley Perry, is remembered as a passionate and dedicated advocate for Aboriginal rights and welfare. She was a founding member of the Aboriginal Legal Service, the Aboriginal Medical Service, the Aboriginal Tent Embassy, the Aboriginal Children's Service and the Aboriginal Housing Company in Redfern.

Her lifelong career caring and fighting for her community began when her brother was imprisoned. She would visit him regularly, and when he was released she continued to visit, providing support for the other prisoners. When asked what her relation to a prisoner was, she would say, 'I'm his mum' – and so she became 'Mum Shirl'. She would provide guidance and support to prisoners who were unfamiliar with the legal system.

While money was tight, she always used what she had to care for others in her community. When parents were unable to care for their children, she found homes for them. She also helped reunite separated children with their parents. If she couldn't find a home for a particular child she would take them in herself – it is estimated she raised 60 children. Mum Shirl shows just how limitless a mother's love can be.

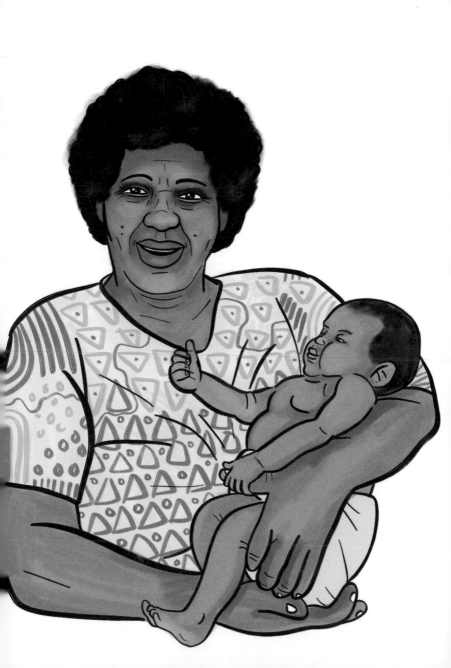

Serena Williams

TENNIS CHAMPION

Serena Williams

'Most of you moms deal with the same thing. Whether stay-at-home or working, finding that balance with kids is a true art. You are the true heroes.'

- SERENA ON INSTAGRAM

On 28 January 2017, international tennis star Serena Williams won the Australian Open, claiming her 23rd Grand Slam singles title. What fans didn't know was that Serena was actually eight weeks pregnant when she won. Serena and her husband welcomed their first child in September 2017. She has since opened up about suffering postnatal depression, describing the feelings of inadequacy she experienced as she came to terms with her new role as a mother. It's hard to believe the tennis star could ever feel anything other than badass, but her honesty reveals the struggles so many mothers around the world face.

As one of the most accomplished tennis players of the century, Serena could have retired as a living legend, but her drive to kick tennis butt was strong. 'There's something really attractive about the idea of moving to San Francisco and just being a mom,' she said. 'But not yet. It needs to be said in a powerful way: I want more Grand Slams.'

However, Serena's return to tennis wasn't all smooth sailing. After officials at the French Open tried to ban her specialised cat suit, which helped prevent blood clots, Serena was vocal about the way female athlete's bodies are policed and held to outdated dress standards. She responded to the ban by wearing a tutu in her next match and won in straight sets. Stylish and badass – what a woman.

Nancy Edison

EDUCATOR

Nancy Edison

'My mother was the making of me. She was so true, so sure of me; and I felt I had something to live for, someone I must not disappoint.'

- THOMAS EDISON

....

The youngest of Nancy Edison's seven kids was Thomas Alva Edison, who would go on to become one of the world's most well-known inventors. Despite his later success, Thomas struggled at school. A devout Presbyterian, Nancy had some formal education and put this to good use after Thomas's teacher deemed him 'addled' – a term used in the 1800's to refer to people with a developmental or learning disability.

Understanding that some children simply learn differently to others, Nancy became a passionate advocate for her son, believing that he could flourish in the right environment, and decided to continue his education at home. She was a devoted and dedicated teacher, choosing to focus on her son's strengths rather than his weaknesses. It was her sympathetic understanding of Thomas's learning abilities that bred confidence and allowed him to go on to become a prominent inventor.

Without his mother's perseverance and dedication, Thomas Edison may not have become a household name.

Jane Goodall

PRIMATOLOGIST

Jane Goodall

'When you meet chimps you meet individual personalities. When a baby chimp looks at you it's just like a human baby. We have a responsibility to them.'

– JANE INTERVIEWED IN THE *GUARDIAN*

Jane Goodall is known for her ground-breaking research on chimpanzee behaviour, and is one of the few female scientists who is a household name. But her incredible scientific career could very easily not have eventuated. As a little girl she was passionate about animals and longed to travel to Africa, but many people laughed at her dreams: 'I was supposed to be a secretary in Bournemouth.'

In the 1960s, at a time when women where not encouraged to explore or take up intensive scientific research, Jane embarked on a daring expedition to Gombe, Tanzania, with one goal in mind: understanding the chimpanzee community. Day after day she sat and observed the incredible animals, until the chimps gradually accepted her into their community. By spending years living with chimps she became one of the first researchers to notice their intelligence, emotional capacity and familial bonds.

Jane dedicated her life to protecting and understanding chimpanzees. Her love for them is like a mother's, and she fights to protect them from extinction through conservation organisation the Jane Goodall Institute and the Roots & Shoots programme, which encourages young people to be involved in the environment. Her son, affectionately nicknamed Grub, spent many years of his childhood in rainforests surrounded by his chimpanzee family, proving that a scientific career and motherhood can go hand in hand.

JK Rowling

WRITER & MUGGLE

JK Rowling

'I am prouder of my years as a single mother than of any other part of my life.'

- JK IN A PIECE WRITTEN FOR HER ORGANISATION, GINGERBREAD

....

Joanne 'JK' Rowling, the author behind the literary sensation that inspired a generation of avid readers and shaped the childhoods of many, wrote the first four Harry Potter books as a single mother. She faced ongoing rejection from publishing houses, and for years relied on government assistance while she struggled to find stable employment. But success was just around the corner, and when the Harry Potter books were finally picked up by Bloomsbury, they earned approximately $480 million in their first three years on the shelves.

While JK is now one of the richest authors alive and is happily remarried, the stigmatisation of single parents, and particularly the difficulty they face getting back into the job market, are issues that remain close to her heart. JK now serves as the president of Gingerbread, an organisation that provides support to single parents and their children.

JK Rowling could have pretended that her years of struggle never happened, but she uses her status to give hope to single parents and help lift them out of poverty, which is more inspiring and badass than any spell cast at Hogwarts!

Ameera Ahmad Harouda

WAR CORRESPONDENT

Ameera Ahmad Harouda

'During the time of war, the hardest part for me is ...
leaving my children. [But] I'm proud that I can tell you
stories, sad and happy, stories about my small corner
of the world, Gaza.'

– AMEERA IN HER TED TALK

When Ameera Ahmad Harouda hears the sounds of bombs falling and buildings crashing to the ground, she heads straight towards the destruction: 'I want to be there first, because these stories should be told.'

Living in the Gaza Strip, one of the world's most dangerous and unstable areas, does not make life easy for Ameera, who has young children and a husband. Neither does her job as a 'fixer' – a local guide who leads foreign correspondents into the heart of political turmoil, helping them to expose the devastating chaos of war.

As the first female fixer in the Gaza area, Ameera is the woman behind the byline of some of the most compelling news stories and war reports. 'When the violence escalates, Ameera Ahmad Harouda is the "go-to" news fixer,' said the BBC. Ameera has worked for the BBC and CNN during the Israel-Gaza conflict, and was instrumental in the release of kidnapped British journalist Alan Johnston, all accomplished while raising two young children.

You may not see her face on the TV, or notice her name in the newspapers, but Ameera is an incredible woman and mother who deserves to be celebrated – the perfect example of a badass mum!

Valentina Tereshkova

COSMONAUT

Valentina Tereshkova

'If women can be railroad workers in Russia, why can't they fly in space?'
– VALENTINA IN THE RUSSIAN WEEKLY *OGONYOK*

In the midst of the 'space-race' era, Russia's Valentina Tereshkova became the first woman to travel to space.

Valentina left school at just 16, but continued her education through correspondence courses. A skydiving enthusiast, she later volunteered for the Soviet space program, where she was accepted as a cosmonaut. After more than a year of intense training, Valentina was chosen to pilot the Vostok 6 spaceflight. On 16 June 1963, Vostok launched with Valentina at the helm. She orbited the earth 48 times over a three-day period. Her journey was closely followed by TV viewers in the Soviet Union and Europe who watched, transfixed, as she floated in space.

Following her flight, Valentina married fellow cosmonaut Andriyan Nikolayev, and their daughter, Elena, was the first person born to parents who had both been into space. Valentina remained active in the space community, and regularly dismissed the notion that women couldn't work and be mothers: 'I strongly feel that no work done by a woman in the field of science or culture or whatever, however vigorous or demanding, can enter into conflict with her craving for the bliss of motherhood. On the contrary, these two aspects of her life can complement each other perfectly.'

Cate Blanchett

ACTRESS

Cate Blanchett

'I like being able to be the kind of mother who is not only there to take care of [my children] ... but also one who has a career.'

– CATE INTERVIEWED IN WORKING MOTHER MAGAZINE

Cate Blanchett, one of the most accomplished actors in Australia, won't stand for the double standards mothers face. As the mother of four children, she frequently calls out harmful representations of mothers in Hollywood and urges the media to ask themselves: would you ask a father the same question? '"How do you balance? How do you have it all?" ... It's certainly a question that's never asked of men,' she said at a press conference.

Fame is not wasted on Cate; she uses it as a platform to give voice to the people who need it the most. She has been appointed as an ambassador for the Australian Conservation Foundation, the Australian Film Institute and the United Nations High Commissioner for Refugees. More recently, she marched up the steps of the Palais in Cannes alongside 81 female film makers to promote gender equality in the film industry. 'As women, we all face our own unique challenges, but we stand together on these stairs today as a symbol of our determination and commitment to progress,' she told the crowd gathered for the Cannes Film Festival.

Her list of awards is so staggeringly long that it would be impossible to fit it into this book. Needless to say, Cate continues to wow us all with her ability to uplift the arts community in Australia and the wider world. Her grace, strength and commitment to her children and her career makes her a motherly force to be reckoned with.

Amanda Palmer

MUSICIAN

Amanda Palmer

'All I can do is look at the female heroes who've preceded me and NOT descended into crappy boringness and pray to the holy trinity: Patti, Ani, Björki ... hear my prayer. May I not get fucking boring.'

- AMANDA, IN HER OPEN LETTER ON MEDIUM

As a rock musician and outspoken feminist, Amanda Palmer has defied convention in her work and in her personal life. Amanda rose to fame with indie rock music duo The Dresden Dolls and as a solo artist with the release of her album *Who Killed Amanda Palmer*.

When she decided, at 39, to have a child, Amanda received a letter from a concerned fan who felt that her career would suffer: 'When you have this baby, either him/her/it will suffer, or your career will suffer.' In response, Amanda wrote a courageous and startlingly honest open letter where she revealed the complex feelings she had towards her pregnancy and admitted that she too had trouble equating 'mother' with 'artist'. 'Imagining my female idols as mother was a completely squirmy idea. Rock stars and artists did not ... mom,' she wrote.

Amanda wrote frankly about her fears: the fear of losing her identity as an artist, of become boring and irrelevant, and of having to sacrifice her bohemian lifestyle. But in the end she drew inspiration from the long list of incredible women who are mothers *and* artists such as Patti Smith, Björk and Ani DiFranco. Amanda's son, Anthony, was born on 16 September 2015, and since then she has continued to create art and music that is both unique and inspiring, and irreverent and badass.

Fanny Blankers-Koen

OLYPMIAN

Fanny—Blankers-Koen

'One newspaperman wrote that I was too old to run, that I should stay at home and take care of my children ... I said: "I'll show you."'

– FANNY INTERVIEWED IN *THE NEW YORK TIMES*

....

Known as the 'Flying Housewife', the pioneering track athlete Fanny Blankers-Koen remains the only woman to win four gold medals in track and field at a single Olympics.

Fanny made her Olympic debut at age 18 during the 1936 Berlin Games, in spite of the widely held view that women should not compete in sports. When she gave birth to her first child in 1942 many assumed her career as an athlete was over. But Fanny had other ideas, resuming training only weeks after the birth of her son.

At 30 years of age, now with two young children in tow, Fanny announced her intentions to compete in the 1948 London Games. She was subject to heavy public scrutiny both for her age and for continuing to race as a mother: 'I got very many bad letters, people writing that I must stay home with my children and that I should not be allowed to run on a track with ... short trousers.' The disapproval she faced only made Fanny more determined to prove her critics wrong. And so she did, winning an amazing four gold medals! In an era where gender roles and images of motherhood were very rigid, Fanny's victories at the London Games helped dispel the myth that being a mother and a wife automatically ruled out a woman's capability beyond those roles.

Angie Xtravaganza

MOTHER TO THE HOUSE OF XTRAVAGANZA

Angie Xtravaganza

'A mother is one who raises a child, not one who borns it.'

....

As 'house mother' at the House of Xtravaganza, and mother to dozens of LGBTQ+ children and adults who were rejected by society, Angie Xtravaganza demonstrates that motherhood is what you make of it.

Not a lot is known about Angie's early life, just that she arrived on the streets of New York at the age of 13. Before she was 20 she joined the House of Xtravaganza, one of the most well-known 'houses' in the underground ballroom scene in New York. Houses provided surrogate families for gay, gender nonconforming and transgender youth and were run by a 'house father' and 'house mother'. As mother to the House of Xtravaganza, Angie cared for all its members, guiding them through the world of the 1980s New York ballroom scene. These ballrooms were places of acceptance, security and celebration for LGBTQ+ people of all ages; the scene is most famous for creating the voguing dance style and being the subject of the *Paris is Burning* documentary.

Angie Xtravagana died at only 28 years of age, but her legacy lives on through the House of Xtravaganza, which is still a vibrant and flourishing family today. Angie's reinvention of motherhood shows that biology is not the only thing that determines a family; the love of those who appreciate and support you makes for the best type of family.

Jacinda Ardern

NEW ZEALAND'S 40TH PRIME MINISTER

Jacinda Ardern

'I am not the first woman to multi-task. I am not the first woman to work and have a baby – there are many women who have done this before.'

– JACINDA IN AN INTERVIEW WITH RADIO NEW ZEALAND

Elected New Zealand's 40th Prime Minister on 26 October 2017, Jacinda Ardern is the country's youngest prime minister in over 150 years. On 21 July 2018, she broke another record when she welcomed Neve Te Aroha into the world – becoming only the second elected head of government to give birth while in office.

Jacinda and her partner, Clarke Gayford, discovered she was pregnant between winning the election and taking office. Following the announcement of her pregnancy, Jacinda challenged entrenched gender ideas of leadership and motherhood. When a stroppy *Daily Mail* columnist wrote that 'a pregnant Prime Minister isn't feminism ... a country shouldn't have to compete for your attention with a colaccy toddler', Jacinda replied with an unimpressed 'eh'. 'I'm pregnant, not incapacitated,' she retorted.

'I'll be a Prime Minister and a mum,' she said upon returning to work six weeks after giving birth to her daughter. In September 2018, little Neve became the first infant ever to attend the United Nations General Assembly, where her security pass dubbed her the 'First Baby' of New Zealand. Jacinda's determination and conviction to be a leader and a mother in her own unique way makes her the epitome of a badass mum.

Sarah Firth is a comic artist, writer, graphic recorder and animator based in Melbourne. She has received a Frankie Magazine Good Stuff Award, was a finalist in the Incinerator Social Change Art Award, and her graphic essay on complexity was listed in *The Conversation*'s ten best literary comics in Australia. She has a fat stack of self-published comics and pieces in upcoming anthologies with Abrams Books, Picador and Allen & Unwin. She is currently working on her debut graphic novel thanks to the Creators Fund program.